This book belongs to

Password Tracker

WEBSITE

@

👤

🔒

WEBSITE

@

👤

🔒

WEBSITE

@

👤

🔒

Password Tracker

WEBSITE

@

👤

🔒

WEBSITE

@

👤

🔒

WEBSITE

@

👤

🔒

Password Tracker

WEBSITE

@

&

🔒

WEBSITE

@

&

🔒

WEBSITE

@

&

🔒

Password Tracker

WEBSITE

@

🔒

WEBSITE

@
👤
🔒

WEBSITE

@
👤
🔒

Password Tracker

WEBSITE

@

👤

🔒

WEBSITE

@

👤

🔒

WEBSITE

@

👤

🔒

Password Tracker

WEBSITE

@

👤

🔒

WEBSITE

@

👤

🔒

WEBSITE

@

👤

🔒

Password Tracker

WEBSITE

@

👤

🔒

WEBSITE

@

👤

🔒

WEBSITE

@

👤

🔒

Password Tracker

WEBSITE

@
👤
🔒

WEBSITE

@
👤
🔒

WEBSITE

@
👤
🔒

Password Tracker

WEBSITE

@
&
🔒

WEBSITE

@
&
🔒

WEBSITE

@
&
🔒

Password Tracker

WEBSITE

@

🔒

WEBSITE

@

👤

🔒

WEBSITE

@

👤

🔒

Password Tracker

WEBSITE

@

👤

🔒

WEBSITE

@

👤

🔒

WEBSITE

@

👤

🔒

Password Tracker

WEBSITE

@

  👤

  🔒

WEBSITE

@

  👤

  🔒

WEBSITE

@

  👤

  🔒

Password Tracker

WEBSITE

@
👤
🔒

WEBSITE

@
👤
🔒

WEBSITE

@
👤
🔒

Password Tracker

WEBSITE

@

👤

🔒

WEBSITE

@

👤

🔒

WEBSITE

@

👤

🔒

Password Tracker

WEBSITE

@

👤

🔒

WEBSITE

@

👤

🔒

WEBSITE

@

👤

🔒

Password Tracker

WEBSITE

@
👤
🔒

WEBSITE

@
👤
🔒

WEBSITE

@
👤
🔒

Password Tracker

WEBSITE

@

👤

🔒

WEBSITE

@

👤

🔒

WEBSITE

@

👤

🔒

Password Tracker

WEBSITE

@
👤
🔒

WEBSITE

@
👤
🔒

WEBSITE

@
👤
🔒

Password Tracker

WEBSITE

@

👤

🔒

WEBSITE

@

👤

🔒

WEBSITE

@

👤

🔒

Password Tracker

WEBSITE

@

👤

🔒

WEBSITE

@

👤

🔒

WEBSITE

@

👤

🔒

Password Tracker

WEBSITE

@

👤

🔒

WEBSITE

@

👤

🔒

WEBSITE

@

👤

🔒

Password Tracker

WEBSITE

@

👤

🔒

WEBSITE

@

👤

🔒

WEBSITE

@

👤

🔒

Password tracker

WEBSITE

@
  👤
  🔒

WEBSITE

@
  👤
  🔒

WEBSITE

@
  👤
  🔒

Password Tracker

| WEBSITE |

@
👤
🔒

| WEBSITE |

@
👤
🔒

| WEBSITE |

@
👤
🔒

Password Tracker

WEBSITE

@
👤
🔒

WEBSITE

@
👤
🔒

WEBSITE

@
👤
🔒

Password Tracker

WEBSITE

@
👤
🔒

WEBSITE

@
👤
🔒

WEBSITE

@
👤
🔒

Password Tracker

WEBSITE

@
👤
🔒

WEBSITE

@
👤
🔒

WEBSITE

@
👤
🔒

Password Tracker

| WEBSITE |

@
👤
🔒

| WEBSITE |

@
👤
🔒

| WEBSITE |

@
👤
🔒

Password Tracker

WEBSITE

@
👤
🔒

WEBSITE

@
👤
🔒

WEBSITE

@
👤
🔒

Password Tracker

WEBSITE

@

👤

🔒

WEBSITE

@

👤

🔒

WEBSITE

@

👤

🔒

Password Tracker

WEBSITE

@
👤
🔒

WEBSITE

@
👤
🔒

WEBSITE

@
👤
🔒

Password Tracker

WEBSITE

@

👤

🔒

WEBSITE

@

👤

🔒

WEBSITE

@

👤

🔒

Password Tracker

WEBSITE

WEBSITE

WEBSITE

Password Tracker

WEBSITE

@
👤
🔒

WEBSITE

@
👤
🔒

WEBSITE

@
👤
🔒

Password Tracker

WEBSITE

WEBSITE

WEBSITE

Password Tracker

WEBSITE

@

👤

🔒

WEBSITE

@

👤

🔒

WEBSITE

@

👤

🔒

Password Tracker

WEBSITE

@

👤

🔒

WEBSITE

@

👤

🔒

WEBSITE

@

👤

🔒

Password Tracker

WEBSITE

@
👤
🔒

WEBSITE

@
👤
🔒

WEBSITE

@
👤
🔒

Password Tracker

WEBSITE

@

👤

🔒

WEBSITE

@

👤

🔒

WEBSITE

@

👤

🔒

Password Tracker

WEBSITE

@

&

🔒

WEBSITE

@

&

🔒

WEBSITE

@

&

🔒

Password Tracker

| WEBSITE |

@
&
🔒

| WEBSITE |

@
&
🔒

| WEBSITE |

@
&
🔒

Password Tracker

WEBSITE

@

👤

🔒

WEBSITE

@

👤

🔒

WEBSITE

@

👤

🔒

Password Tracker

WEBSITE

@

👤

🔒

WEBSITE

@

👤

🔒

WEBSITE

@

👤

🔒

Password Tracker

WEBSITE

@
👤
🔒

WEBSITE

@
👤
🔒

WEBSITE

@
👤
🔒

Password Tracker

WEBSITE

@

🔒

WEBSITE

@
👤
🔒

WEBSITE

@
👤
🔒

Password Tracker

WEBSITE

@

👤

🔒

WEBSITE

@

👤

🔒

WEBSITE

@

👤

🔒

Password Tracker

WEBSITE

@

👤

🔒

WEBSITE

@

👤

🔒

WEBSITE

@

👤

🔒

Password Tracker

WEBSITE

@
👤
🔒

WEBSITE

@
👤
🔒

WEBSITE

@
👤
🔒

Password Tracker

WEBSITE

@

👤

🔒

WEBSITE

@

👤

🔒

WEBSITE

@

👤

🔒

Password Tracker

WEBSITE

@

👤

🔒

WEBSITE

@

👤

🔒

WEBSITE

@

👤

🔒

Password Tracker

WEBSITE

@

👤

🔒

WEBSITE

@

👤

🔒

WEBSITE

@

👤

🔒

Password Tracker

WEBSITE

@

👤

🔒

WEBSITE

@

👤

🔒

WEBSITE

@

👤

🔒

Password Tracker

WEBSITE

@
👤
🔒

WEBSITE

@
👤
🔒

WEBSITE

@
👤
🔒

Password Tracker

WEBSITE

@
👤
🔒

WEBSITE

@
👤
🔒

WEBSITE

@
👤
🔒

Password Tracker

WEBSITE

@

👤

🔒

WEBSITE

@

👤

🔒

WEBSITE

@

👤

🔒

Password Tracker

WEBSITE

@

👤

🔒

WEBSITE

@

👤

🔒

WEBSITE

@

👤

🔒

Password Tracker

WEBSITE

@
👤
🔒

WEBSITE

@
👤
🔒

WEBSITE

@
👤
🔒

Password Tracker

WEBSITE

@

👤

🔒

WEBSITE

@

👤

🔒

WEBSITE

@

👤

🔒

Password Tracker

WEBSITE

@
👤
🔒

WEBSITE

@
👤
🔒

WEBSITE

@
👤
🔒

Password Tracker

WEBSITE

@

👤

🔒

WEBSITE

@

👤

🔒

WEBSITE

@

👤

🔒

Password Tracker

WEBSITE

@
👤
🔒

WEBSITE

@
👤
🔒

WEBSITE

@
👤
🔒

Password Tracker

WEBSITE

@

👤

🔒

WEBSITE

@

👤

🔒

WEBSITE

@

👤

🔒

Password Tracker

WEBSITE

 @

🔒

WEBSITE

 @

🔒

WEBSITE

 @

🔒

Password Tracker

WEBSITE

@

👤

🔒

WEBSITE

@

👤

🔒

WEBSITE

@

👤

🔒

Password Tracker

WEBSITE

@

👤

🔒

WEBSITE

@

👤

🔒

WEBSITE

@

👤

🔒

Password Tracker

WEBSITE

@

👤

🔒

WEBSITE

@

👤

🔒

WEBSITE

@

👤

🔒

Password Tracker

WEBSITE

@
👤
🔒

WEBSITE

@
👤
🔒

WEBSITE

@
👤
🔒

Password Tracker

WEBSITE

@

👤

🔒

WEBSITE

@

👤

🔒

WEBSITE

@

👤

🔒

Password Tracker

WEBSITE

@
👤
🔒

WEBSITE

@
👤
🔒

WEBSITE

@
👤
🔒

Password Tracker

WEBSITE

@

👤

🔒

WEBSITE

@

👤

🔒

WEBSITE

@

👤

🔒

Password tracker

| WEBSITE |

@
👤
🔒

| WEBSITE |

@
👤
🔒

| WEBSITE |

@
👤
🔒

Password Tracker

WEBSITE

@

👤

🔒

WEBSITE

@

👤

🔒

WEBSITE

@

👤

🔒

Password Tracker

WEBSITE

@

👤

🔒

WEBSITE

@

👤

🔒

WEBSITE

@

👤

🔒

Password Tracker

WEBSITE

@

👤

🔒

WEBSITE

@

👤

🔒

WEBSITE

@

👤

🔒

Password Tracker

WEBSITE

@

♟

🔒

WEBSITE

@

♟

🔒

WEBSITE

@

♟

🔒

Password Tracker

WEBSITE

@

👤

🔒

WEBSITE

@

👤

🔒

WEBSITE

@

👤

🔒

Password tracker

WEBSITE

WEBSITE

WEBSITE

Password Tracker

WEBSITE

@

👤

🔒

WEBSITE

@

👤

🔒

WEBSITE

@

👤

🔒

Password Tracker

WEBSITE

@
👤
🔒

WEBSITE

@
👤
🔒

WEBSITE

@
👤
🔒

Password Tracker

WEBSITE

@

👤

🔒

WEBSITE

@

👤

🔒

WEBSITE

@

👤

🔒

Password Tracker

WEBSITE

@

👤

🔒

WEBSITE

@

👤

🔒

WEBSITE

@

👤

🔒

Password Tracker

| WEBSITE |

@

👤

🔒

| WEBSITE |

@

👤

🔒

| WEBSITE |

@

👤

🔒

Password Tracker

WEBSITE

@
👤
🔒

WEBSITE

@
👤
🔒

WEBSITE

@
👤
🔒

Password Tracker

WEBSITE

@

👤

🔒

WEBSITE

@

👤

🔒

WEBSITE

@

👤

🔒

Password Tracker

WEBSITE

@
👤
🔒

WEBSITE

@
👤
🔒

WEBSITE

@
👤
🔒

Password Tracker

WEBSITE

@

👤

🔒

WEBSITE

@

👤

🔒

WEBSITE

@

👤

🔒

Password Tracker

WEBSITE

@

WEBSITE

@

WEBSITE

@

Password Tracker

WEBSITE

@

👤

🔒

WEBSITE

@

👤

🔒

WEBSITE

@

👤

🔒

Password Tracker

WEBSITE

@
👤
🔒

WEBSITE

@
👤
🔒

WEBSITE

@
👤
🔒

Password Tracker

WEBSITE

@
👤
🔒

WEBSITE

@
👤
🔒

WEBSITE

@
👤
🔒

Password Tracker

WEBSITE

@

👤

🔒

WEBSITE

@

👤

🔒

WEBSITE

@

👤

🔒

Password Tracker

WEBSITE

WEBSITE

WEBSITE

Password Tracker

WEBSITE

@
👤
🔒

WEBSITE

@
👤
🔒

WEBSITE

@
👤
🔒

Password Tracker

WEBSITE

@

👤

🔒

WEBSITE

@

👤

🔒

WEBSITE

@

👤

🔒

Password tracker

@

👤

🔒

@

👤

🔒

@

👤

🔒

Password Tracker

WEBSITE

@

  👤

  🔒

WEBSITE

@

  👤

  🔒

WEBSITE

@

  👤

  🔒

Password Tracker

WEBSITE

@

👤

🔒

WEBSITE

@

👤

🔒

WEBSITE

@

👤

🔒

Password Tracker

WEBSITE

@

👤

🔒

WEBSITE

@

👤

🔒

WEBSITE

@

👤

🔒

Password Tracker

WEBSITE

WEBSITE

@

WEBSITE

@

Password Tracker

WEBSITE

@
👤
🔒

WEBSITE

@
👤
🔒

WEBSITE

@
👤
🔒

Password Tracker

WEBSITE

@

👤

🔒

WEBSITE

@

👤

🔒

WEBSITE

@

👤

🔒

Password Tracker

WEBSITE

@

👤

🔒

WEBSITE

@

👤

🔒

WEBSITE

@

👤

🔒

Password Tracker

WEBSITE

@

WEBSITE

@

WEBSITE

@

Password Tracker

WEBSITE

@

👤

🔒

WEBSITE

@

👤

🔒

WEBSITE

@

👤

🔒

Password Tracker

WEBSITE

@

WEBSITE

@

WEBSITE

@

Password Tracker

WEBSITE

@

👤

🔒

WEBSITE

@

👤

🔒

WEBSITE

@

👤

🔒

Password Tracker

WEBSITE

WEBSITE

WEBSITE

Password Tracker

WEBSITE

@

👤

🔒

WEBSITE

@

👤

🔒

WEBSITE

@

👤

🔒

Password Tracker

WEBSITE

WEBSITE

WEBSITE

Password Tracker

WEBSITE

@

👤

🔒

WEBSITE

@

👤

🔒

WEBSITE

@

👤

🔒

Password Tracker

WEBSITE

@

👤

🔒

WEBSITE

@

👤

🔒

WEBSITE

@

👤

🔒

Password Tracker

WEBSITE

@

👤

🔒

WEBSITE

@

👤

🔒

WEBSITE

@

👤

🔒

Password Tracker

WEBSITE

@
👤
🔒

WEBSITE

@
👤
🔒

WEBSITE

@
👤
🔒

Password Tracker

WEBSITE

@
👤
🔒

WEBSITE

@
👤
🔒

WEBSITE

@
👤
🔒

Password Tracker

WEBSITE

@
👤
🔒

WEBSITE

@
👤
🔒

WEBSITE

@
👤
🔒

Password Tracker

| WEBSITE |

@

👤

🔒

| WEBSITE |

@

👤

🔒

| WEBSITE |

@

👤

🔒

Password Tracker

WEBSITE

WEBSITE

WEBSITE

Password Tracker

WEBSITE

@

👤

🔒

WEBSITE

@

👤

🔒

WEBSITE

@

👤

🔒

Password tracker

@

👤

🔒

@

👤

🔒

@

👤

🔒

www.ingramcontent.com/pod-product-compliance
Lightning Source LLC
Chambersburg PA
CBHW071255050326
40690CB00011B/2410